Zap!

By

Querida Lu Ahn Funck

The End

Hi! My name is Fluffy.

I'm a Newfoundland, and I'm fascinated with static electricity.

Do you know what static electricity is? Static electricity is the build-up of electricity on the surface of an object. Like when you rub your socks on the carpet or rub a balloon on your hair!

Electrical charges can be "negative" or "positive" but they can't be both, and they can't be in the same place. When they get too close, they trade places causing a shock.

Sometimes it can be a <u>big</u> shock, and you might see a tiny bolt of electricity flash just when the charges change places.

Have your pant legs ever stuck to your sock? Has your hair ever stood up on end when you've gone down a slide? Have you ever touched a doorknob in the winter and gotten a shock?

These are all examples of static electricity.

Fluffy

I hope you enjoy your time with
Zap!

Please consider leaving a review on
Goodreads and
Share this book with a friend!

Bonus materials are available on
www.dreamtimeillustrations.com

Be sure to check it out!

www.ingramcontent.com/pod-product-compliance
Lightning Source LLC
Chambersburg PA
CBHW040513150626
46551CB00033B/2634